We Belong Together

HOLLY POND HILL
BY SUSAN WHEELER

HARVEST HOUSE PUBLISHERS
Eugene, Oregon

We Belong Together

Text Copyright © 2001 by Harvest House Publishers
Eugene, Oregon 97402

ISBN 0-7369-0510-3

Design and production by Garborg Design Works, Minneapolis, Minnesota

Harvest House Publishers has made every effort to trace the ownership of all poems and quotes. In the event of a question arising from the use of a poem or quote, we regret any error made and will be pleased to make the necessary correction in future editions of this book.

Scriptures are taken from the Living Bible, © 1971. Used by permission of Tyndale House Publishers, Inc., Wheaton Illinois 60189.

Printed in Hong Kong.

01 02 03 04 05 06 07 08 09 10 / NG / 10 9 8 7 6 5 4 3 2 1

Come live in my heart
and pay no rent.

SAMUEL LOVER

3

A heart that loves is always young.

GREEK PROVERB

Hereafter in a better world than this, I shall desire more love and knowledge of you.

WILLIAM SHAKESPEARE

5

*W*hoso loves
Believes the impossible.

ELIZABETH BARRETT BROWNING

If you love someone, you will
be loyal to him no matter what
the cost. You will always
believe in him, always expect
the best of him ...

THE BOOK OF 1 CORINTHIANS

To love

and be

loved is to

feel the

sun from

both sides.

DAVID VISCOTT

WHERE

LOVE IS

CONCERNED,

TOO MUCH IS

NOT EVEN

ENOUGH.

PIERRE DE
BEAUMARCHAIS

For a moment Anne hesitated. She had an odd, newly awakened consciousness under all her outraged dignity that the half-shy, half-eager expression in Gilbert's hazel eyes was something that was very good to see. Her heart gave a quick, queer little beat.

L. M. MONTGOMERY
Anne of Green Gables

Nobody has ever measured, not even

poets, how much the heart can hold.

ZELDA FITZGERALD

I would love to spend all my time writing to you; I'd love to share with you all that goes through my mind, all that weighs on my heart, all that gives air to my soul.

LUIGI PIRANDELLO

L ove can never grow old. Locks may lose their brown and gold. Cheeks may fade and hollow grow. But the hearts that love will know, never winter's frost and chill, summer's warmth is in them still.

LEO BUSCAGLIA

The way you let your hand rest in mine, my bewitching Sweetheart, fills me with happiness. It is the perfection of confiding love. Everything you do, the little unconscious things in particular, charms me and increases my sense of nearness to you, identification with you, till my heart is full to overflowing.

WOODROW WILSON

Love is a force more formidable than any other. It is invisible—it cannot be seen or measured, yet it is powerful enough to transform you in a moment, and offer you more joy than any material possession could.

BARBARA DE ANGELIS

Being with you is
like walking on a
very clear morning—
definitely the sensation
of belonging there.

E. B. WHITE

The hours I spend with you I look upon
as sort of a perfumed garden, a dim twilight,
and a fountain singing to it . . . you and you
alone make me feel that I am alive . . .

Other men it is said have

seen angels, but I have

seen thee and thou

art enough.

GEORGE MOORE

Somewhere there's someone who dreams of your smile, and finds in your presence that life is worthwhile, so when you are lonely, remember this is true: Somebody, somewhere is thinking of you.

AUTHOR UNKNOWN

The loving are the daring.

BAYARD TAYLOR

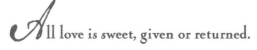

*A*ll love is sweet, given or returned.

PERCY BYSSHE SHELLEY

Two souls with but a single thought,
two hearts that beat as one.

JOHN KEATS

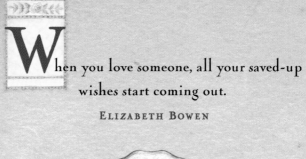

When you love someone, all your saved-up
wishes start coming out.

ELIZABETH BOWEN

Grow old along with
me! The best is
yet to be...

ROBERT BROWNING

To
Someone
very
dear

Susan Wheeler

$\mathcal{L}ove\ is\ th$

I LOVE YOU, NOT ONLY FOR WHAT YOU ARE, BUT FOR WHAT I AM WHEN I AM WITH YOU.

ROY CROFT

beauty of a soul.

ST. AUGUSTINE

Though weary, love is not tired;

Though pressed, it is not straightened;

Though alarmed, it is not confounded.

Love securely passes through all.

THOMAS À KEMPIS

To love is to

receive a glimpse

of heaven.

KAREN SUNDE

JUST

MARRIED

28

Their eyes instantly met,
and the cheeks of each were
overspread with the deepest blush.

JANE AUSTEN
Pride and Prejudice

*Love is the best
thing in the
world, and the
thing that
lives longest.*

HENRY VAN DYKE

29

Love is like a tranquil
breeze that sweeps over my
soul making me whole.

AUTHOR UNKNOWN

The best and most
beautiful things in the
world cannot be seen or
even touched. They must
be felt with the heart.

HELEN KELLER

Gravity cannot
be held
responsible for
people falling
in love.

ALBERT EINSTEIN

LOVE KEEPS

THE HEART

WARM.

AUTHOR UNKNOWN

Romans 3:22

I had not intended to love him; the reader knows I had wrought hard to extirpate from my soul the germs of love there detected; and now, at the first renewed view of him, they spontaneously arrived, green and strong! He made me love him without looking at me.

CHARLOTTE BRONTË
Jane Eyre

We are each of us angels with only one wing. And we can only fly embracing each other.

LUCIANO DE CRESCENZO

The giving of love is an education in itself.

ELEANOR ROOSEVELT

The soul that can
speak through the eyes
can also kiss with a gaze.

GUSTAVO ADOLFO
BECQUER

Susan
Wheeler

39

Love is composed of a single soul
inhabiting two bodies.

ARISTOTLE

LOVE IS A
BEAUTIFUL DREAM.

WILLIAM SHARPE

Did my heart love till now?

Forswear it, sight!

For I ne'er saw true

beauty till this night.

WILLIAM SHAKESPEARE

Romeo and Juliet

LOVE IS THE
EMBLEM OF
ETERNITY; IT
CONFOUNDS ALL
NOTION OF TIME:
EFFACES ALL
MEMORY OF A
BEGINNING, ALL
FEAR OF AN END.

MADAME DE STAEL

A loving heart is the
truest wisdom.

CHARLES DICKENS

41

Love might not make the world go round, but it sure makes the ride worthwhile.

AUTHOR UNKNOWN

I love the ground under his feet, and the air over his head, and everything he touches, and every word he says. I love all his looks, and all his actions, and him entirely and altogether.

EMILY BRONTË
Wuthering Heights

Having you I want no other.
All my life is one with yours.

R.D. BLACKMORE
Lorna Doone

Life,

the gift of nature,

Love,

the gift of life,

A Kiss,

the gift of love.

AUTHOR UNKNOWN

A kiss is a lovely trick designed by nature to
stop speech when words become superfluous.

INGRID BERGMAN

*F*or what is love itself, for the
one we love best? An enfolding of
immeasurable cares which yet are better
than any joys outside our love.

GEORGE ELIOT

To keep one sacred flame
Through life unchilled, unmoved,
To love in wintry age, the same
As first in youth we loved,
To feel that we adore
Even to fond excess
That though the heart would break with more,
It could not live with less.

THOMAS MOORE

You are so beautiful,

my love,

in every part of you . . .

THE SONG OF SOLOMON